Pocket Mandala 1

©2015 by Charles Orlik

©2015 Published by CiJiRO Publishing

Introduction:

Thanks for purchasing Pocket Mandala 1 by Charles Orlik. We know you will find this collection of Mandalas a hit for fun on the go. Perfect to pop into your purse or briefcase you can now take coloring fun on the train ride to work, at lunchtime, while you are on a trip, etc. The possibilities are endless.

Are you enjoying this book? Please rate and review on Amazon. I highly appreciate it.

Please keep in touch:

Facebook: https://www.facebook.com/newadultcoloringbooks

Twitter: @coloring_books1

To see my other releases, visit my Amazon Store link:

Web: www.ColoringForGrownUps.Net

www.ingramcontent.com/pod-product-compliance
Lightning Source LLC
Chambersburg PA
CBHW021037180526
45163CB00005B/2164